PATTERNS

FIRST MATHS

©2017
Book Life
King's Lynn
Norfolk PE30 4LS

ISBN: 978-1-78637-123-2

Written by:
Joanna Brundle

Edited by:
Charlie Ogden

Designed by:
Danielle Jones

A catalogue record for this book
is available from the British Library

PHOTO CREDITS

CONTENTS

PAGE 4   Patterns Are Everywhere

PAGE 6   In the Garden

PAGE 8   At Home

PAGE 10   Time

PAGE 12   Shapes

PAGE 14   Spirals

PAGE 16   Stripes

PAGE 18   Patterns in Nature

PAGE 20   Out and About

PAGE 22   Spot the Patterns

PAGE 24   Fun with Patterns

PATTERNS ARE EVERYWHERE

Supermarket trollies in a row make a pattern.

You can see patterns wherever you go.
Patterns are everywhere.

Can you see a pattern on these ice cream cones?

IN THE GARDEN

The petals and seeds on this sunflower make a pattern.

A butterfly has the same pattern on both its wings.

AT HOME

There are patterns in this bathroom.
Can you see them on the floor?

TIME

Which season is this?

Our seasons follow a pattern. It goes spring, summer, autumn and winter.

Your day follows a pattern. You get up in the morning and go to sleep at night.

SHAPES

Look for patterns on this quilt.

Shapes can join together to make patterns.

SPIRALS

Snail
Shells

Snails have a spiral shape on their shells.

This staircase makes a spiral pattern.
Trace the pattern with your finger.

STRIPES

PATTERNS IN NATURE

There are circle patterns on this tree stump.

Look at this honeycomb and the two busy bees.
Can you see any patterns?

19

See if you can spot any patterns on these buildings.

Look out for patterns on the road, like this zebra crossing.

SPOT THE PATTERNS

What patterns can you see?

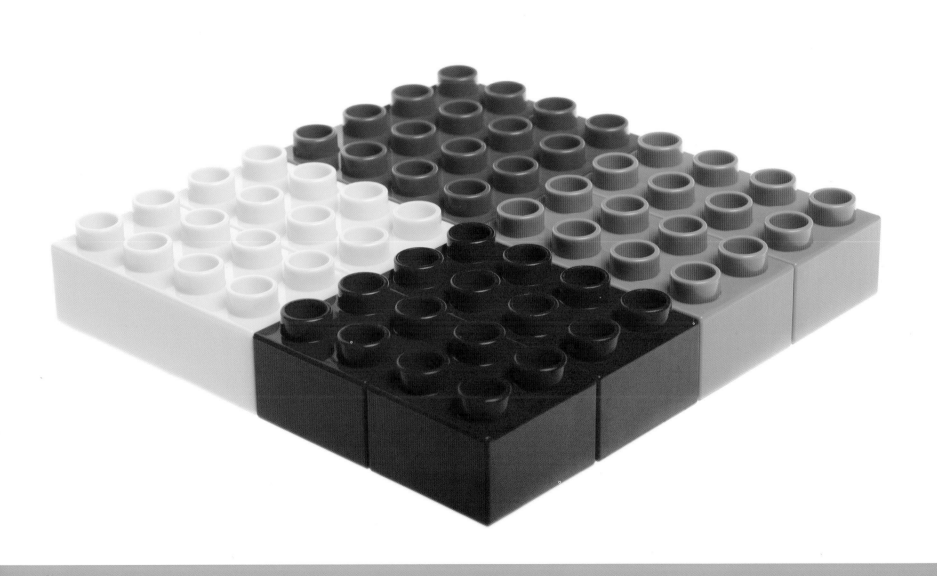

FUN WITH PATTERNS

Try moving in this pattern. Hop, jump, clap, hop, jump, clap!

Try making some patterns of your own!